Before I go to sleep

To Linda and Martin,

On the occasion of your Christening on 20th June, 1976. We wish you God's blessing throughout your lives

Auntie Chris, Uncle Geoff, Neil and David.

Enid Blyton

BEFORE I GO TO SLEEP

A book of Bible stories and prayers for children

———

COLOUR PICTURES BY JANUSZ GRABIANSKI

BLACK AND WHITE DRAWINGS BY
LESLIE WOOD

BROCKHAMPTON PRESS

ISBN 0 340 17528 1

Published in Great Britain 1975 by Brockhampton Press Ltd,
Salisbury Road, Leicester.
This edition copyright © Brockhampton Press Ltd 1975
Printed in Great Britain by Hazell Watson & Viney Ltd, Aylesbury, Bucks.
First published in 1953 in the United States of America
by Little, Brown and Company.
Colour illustrations copyright © 1972, 1973
by Verlag Carl Ueberreuter, Wein. Heidelberg.
All rights reserved.
Black and white illustrations copyright © 1975 Brockhampton Press Ltd.

Contents

How to use this book

In this book you will find a story and a prayer for every day of the month. Begin at the right date, and go on from there. Go back to the beginning when you have reached the last day of the month.

On Christmas Eve, Christmas Day, Good Friday and Easter Sunday read the special story and prayer for those days. You will find them towards the end of the book.

There are also special prayers for special days such as your birthday. Look them up and see what they are – then you can use them when the time comes. Find the Lord's Prayer too, on pages 134 and 135, and read it, and then read exactly what it means, before you learn it.

If you have little brothers or sisters who like stories, tell them any you think they would like.

I hope you will like your bedside book. Look all through it before you begin and see exactly what is in it, so that you will know.

Love from

ENID BLYTON

Stories and prayers
for each day of the month

The first day

The beginning of things

(Genesis i ; ii. 1–7)

In the very beginning of things God thought that it would be good to make a fair and beautiful world. So he began to make it.

There was no day and no night then. Everything was dark and empty. So God said, 'Let there be light!' and there was light. God saw that the light was good, and he divided the light from the darkness and called the light Day and the darkness Night.

In that time great waters covered all the earth. Then God divided them and commanded the land to appear. So there were seas and lands, the sky, and light over everything.

Nothing grew on the mountains or the plains. No birds flew in the sky. Everything was bare and empty; only the wind made a noise, and the waters of the seas.

Then God commanded the grass to cover the earth, and plants to grow, and trees, each bearing its own seeds to cover the earth with beauty.

And they all grew and clothed the earth, and God looked upon them and saw that they were good.

Then God set the sun and the moon in the sky. 'They shall divide the day from the night,' he said. 'They shall give the days and nights, the seasons and the years. Let them give light upon the earth.'

And God also set the stars in the sky, and he saw that what he had done was good.

Then God wanted living creatures on the earth, birds and insects, fish and animals. And he said, 'Let the waters bring forth great numbers of living creatures, and let the sky be full of winged birds.'

Then in the waters grew all sorts of living creatures, both great and small; and the air was full of the sound of wings, as birds flew over the earth, calling to one another, and singing.

Then God thought of the animals that move over the earth. He made the mighty ones and he made those that creep

through the grass. Lions and tigers, elephants and horses, cows and sheep, squirrels and mice, he made them all.

Out of his great love and power he made the robin that sings on the bough, the beetle that hurries through the grass, the lion that roars in the hills, the mouse that trembles in his hole. He made the glowing butterfly and the hurrying ant.

And when God looked at all the things he had made, he took delight in them and saw that they were good. He blessed the world and all its living things, and he commanded them to grow, and to have families, so that the world might be full of the creatures he had made.

And so the flowers made seed that grew into new plants. The birds laid eggs, the animals bore little ones.

Then last of all God made man. He breathed life into him, and made him lord of all the creatures of the earth. And once more God looked at all that he had made, and behold, it was very good.

Prayer

Great Father God, I thank you for this beautiful world you have made. Thank you for the birds that sing so sweetly, and fly so swiftly. Thank you for the flowers with all their scents and colours. Thank you for the lovely butterflies. Thank you for the horses that work for us, the dogs that guard us, the cats that sit by our fireside, the sheep whose wool warms us and the cows who give us milk. Thank you for my father and mother, and for all who love me.

Amen

The beautiful garden

(Genesis ii. 15–17; iii)

The first man that God made was called Adam, and his wife was called Eve. They lived in a beautiful garden that God had made for them, and Adam was lord over all the animals.

'You may go where you like in this garden,' said God, 'and you may eat from any tree you like except one. You must not eat from the tree that is called the Tree of the Knowledge of Good and Evil. You must only know the good and lovely things. Do not eat from that tree or your happiness will go.'

Now one day the great snake that lived in the garden came to Eve, and asked her why she did not eat from the tree that stood in the very midst of the beautiful Garden of Eden.

'I may not,' said Eve. 'God has forbidden it, but I do not know why.'

'He has forbidden it because he knows that if you eat its fruit you will become as great and powerful as he is,' said the wicked serpent. 'See the lovely ripe fruit, Eve. Pick some and eat it. You will become as wise as God himself then!'

So foolish, disobedient Eve picked the fruit and ate some. It was so delicious that she gave some to Adam too, and he ate it with her.

Now God always came to talk with Adam and Eve in their garden in the cool of the day. That evening, when he came, Adam and Eve were afraid, and they hid themselves.

God's voice came on the evening air, 'Adam, where are you?'

Then Adam and Eve crept out from their hiding place and stood before God. 'I heard your voice in the garden and I was afraid,' said Adam. 'I was full of shame and I hid myself.'

'What makes you feel shame and fear?' said God, sternly. 'Have you eaten the fruit of the tree that I commanded you not to eat?'

'Eve gave me the fruit to eat,' said Adam, hanging his head.

'The snake came to me and told me to eat it,' said Eve, trembling and weeping.

Then God turned to the snake. 'You have done a wicked thing,' he said. 'For your punishment you must crawl along the ground, and never shall you be able to lift yourself up.'

The serpent slid away, crawling through the grass. Then God turned to Adam and Eve.

'I gave you all things out of my love,' he told them. 'Only this one tree you were told not to touch. You have spoiled your great happiness. You must go away from this beautiful garden, out into the great world beyond, and you must work hard every day, for as long as you live.'

And so Adam and Eve fled away from the beautiful garden. Sometimes they went back to see if they could look into it and remember the happy days they had spent there.

But they could never enter it. Adam and Eve had lost their garden forever.

Prayer

O Great God, our Father in Heaven, help me to do all the things you wish me to do. Help me to obey your commandments, and to remember your words. When someone tempts me to do wrong, let me remember the snake in the Garden of Eden. Then I shall not listen to wrong things, or be disobedient and foolish.

Let me never be ashamed before you as Adam was, or hide from you in fear, but always seek you in love and trust.

Amen

The third day

Noah's Ark

(Genesis vi. 5–22; vii; viii; ix. 1–17)

Now one day God looked down upon the earth and saw that there was much cruelty and hatred and greed among the men and women there. He was sad that men should have grown so evil.

'I cannot let such things be,' said God. 'I shall send a great flood upon the earth to destroy these evil things. But if I find anything that is good I will save it.'

Now there was one man who loved the Lord God, and was just and good. His name was Noah. God came to him one day and told him that a great flood of water would soon cover the earth.

'But you and your family shall be saved,' God said. 'You must make yourself an ark, a ship of wood. Build rooms inside it, and daub it with pitch so that no water can come in.'

Noah listened in fear and awe. Then he called his three sons to him, and they did as God commanded. They made a great ark of wood, with a door in the side, and a window near the top. There were many rooms in the ark, and there were ladders that led from the lower rooms to those above.

Everyone came to look and laugh. 'Why should you build

18

a ship on dry land, far from any water?' said the people. 'You are mad!'

Before the great flood began Noah took into the ark with him two of every living creature, lions, bears, cats, squirrels, eagles, sparrows and all the rest. He took food, too, and all his family.

Then there came a terrible wind and storm, and the rain fell as it had never fallen before. It rained day and night, and soon deep waters began to cover the earth. The ark floated like a ship, and Noah and his family were glad to be safely inside.

Day after day the rain fell, until water covered the whole earth. Noah fed the animals and birds, and looked into every room to make sure that no water was trickling in from outside.

After forty days and nights, the rain stopped. Noah opened the window and saw the great sea of grey water outside. There was nothing but water to be seen, no trees, no hills, nothing.

Then the waters began to go down and the ark came to rest on the top of a high mountain. The sun came out and the birds in the ark sang loudly for joy.

Noah sent out a dove, but it came back because there was nowhere to perch. He sent it out a second time and it came back with a green leaf. The third time it did not come back at all.

And when the waters had gone from the earth, Noah opened the door of the ark and every creature went out gladly into the sun. Noah and his family went out too, the children skipping gaily over the grass.

Then God made Noah a solemn promise. 'Never again will

I send down waters to flood the earth. See, here is a sign that I will always keep my promise.'

And then a beautiful rainbow gleamed in the sky, made up of all the colours we know.

Prayer

O God, our Heavenly Father, when I see the rainbow in the sky, I will remember how you put it there for Noah. I will remember the terrible time when it rained forty days and nights without stopping.

I will remember that it makes you sad when you see bad things in people's hearts, and when they do wicked and cruel things.

I am only a child but I do not want to make you sad. I will try to be good and I will think often of the words that Jesus, your son, said to us – 'Love one another'.

Amen

Jesus and his twelve friends

(*Matthew iv. 18–20; xvi. 17–18*)

Jesus, who was born in Bethlehem on the first Christmas, became a carpenter, like his father Joseph. But soon he wanted
to do something greater than making tables and mending
wheels.

'I must go out into the countryside and tell the people how
to be good and kind. I must go and heal those who are sick. I
must tell the children stories that will help them to grow up
into fine men and women,' Jesus said to himself.

So he went out to do these things; but he needed people to
help him. 'I must have friends,' he thought. 'I must have fol-
lowers who will teach the same things as I do. Where shall I
find them?'

He went down to the Lake of Galilee. There were always
fishermen there with their boats. Jesus stood by the water,
looking at the busy men.

He saw two brothers at work. They were good fishermen,
and their names were Simon and Andrew. 'They would be
my friends and help me,' thought Jesus, and he called to them
across the blue water.

They looked up and saw him. 'Come with me!' called
Jesus.

Simon and Andrew knew that they must go with this man,

23

whose face was so noble and strong. They pulled in their nets, took up their oars, and rowed to where Jesus stood. 'What do you want us to do?' they asked. 'We will do all you ask!'

Now a little farther along was another boat. In it were three men, two brothers called James and John and their father. All of them were very busy, mending their torn nets.

Jesus called across to the two brothers, 'Come with me!'

And James and John came straight to the shore, eager to follow Jesus. They loved and trusted him, and were glad to be chosen as his friends.

These four were the first friends of Jesus, close to him all his life. He chose eight more after that, but he loved and trusted his first four friends the best.

One of the four was brave, kind, lovable Simon. Some people said that he could not always be trusted, but Jesus knew that Simon was the right friend for him.

He gave Simon a new name. 'I shall not call you Simon,' he said. 'Your name shall be Peter.'

Simon was surprised. 'Why will you call me Peter?' he asked.

'Peter means a rock,' said Jesus. 'I want someone who will be as steady as a rock. I am going to build a great Kingdom of Love, and it must be built on rock so that it will always stand!'

Then, with his twelve friends, Jesus went out into the countryside to talk to the people and to heal them when they were sick. And Peter, the rock, was always with him, loving and kind.

Prayer

Dear Lord Jesus, I know that long ago you chose your good and loving friends to help you in your work.

I want to be your friend and follower too, so please choose me, though I am young and small.

I want to be like Peter, a rock. I will be steady and true.

Say to me as you said to Peter 'Come with me', and I will come. I will be your true friend in all the ways I know.

Amen

The friend of little children

(Mark x. 13–16)

Jesus loved little children, and always welcomed them when they came to him. They took his hand sometimes as he walked along. They climbed on his knee when he sat down.

They told him all the little things that happened to them. 'I have broken my ship. I am very sad.'

'And I have been naughty today, and Mother is cross with me.'

'Look, I have picked this flower. Would you like it?'

That was the kind of thing the children said to Jesus, and he listened to them all. Often he told them stories. He was a wonderful storyteller, and the children listened to every word, getting as close to him as they could.

One day Jesus was preaching in a village, and there were crowds round him as usual. Some of the mothers spoke together.

'Shall we get our children and take them to Jesus? He would put his hands on them, those wonderful hands that heal sick people, and he would bless our little ones.'

'Yes. We will take even our babies,' said the women, and they went to gather their children together.

Soon they had them all, babies in their arms, toddlers clinging to their skirts, and older children eager to see the wonderful preacher.

They pushed their way through the crowds to where Jesus sat. He looked tired, for he had been talking to many people that day. His disciples were round him, anxious that he should now rest a little.

A mother spoke to one of the disciples. 'We want to bring our children to your master. He loves children, and will bless them for us. If only he would put his hands on them it would help our boys and girls to grow up into good men and women.'

'Go away,' said the disciple. 'Jesus is very busy. He cannot see you and your children now.'

'He has been talking to so many people,' said another disciple. 'He needs a rest. He cannot be troubled with children just now. Perhaps later on.'

The mothers were very disappointed. They turned away with sad faces, pulling their children with them.

But Jesus saw their faces, and he knew at once what had happened. He called to his disciples.

'Do not forbid the children to come to me. Bring them here. They belong to the Kingdom of God just as you do. I say to you that unless you have the open heart of a little child, you cannot enter in my Kingdom of Love!'

Then gladly the mothers brought their children to Jesus. He took them into his arms one by one and blessed them with love and tenderness.

'The children can always come to me!' said Jesus. 'They are my friends and I am theirs.'

Prayer

O Lord Jesus, if I had lived in the days when you were on this earth, I could have gone to you and told you all I wanted to. I could have loved you and done little things for you.

But I can still come to you and talk to you. I can tell you the wrong things I have done. I can ask you to help me to put them right. I can ask you to bless me and surround me with your love all day and night. So bless me, Lord Jesus, and take me into your Kingdom of Love.

Amen

The lost sheep

(*Luke xv. 4–7*)

There was once a shepherd who had a hundred sheep in his fold. He knew them all and they knew him.

In the daytime the shepherd let the sheep out of their fold. They wandered away on the hillside to eat, and went to the little stream to drink.

Sometimes they lay down in the sun, half asleep. They did not bother about the wolves, because the shepherd was always nearby to drive them off.

At night the sheep went back to their shepherd, and he led them to the fold. He counted them and shut them in. Now they were safely in the fold, where no wolf could harm them.

One night, when he counted his sheep, the shepherd found that there was one missing. There were only ninety-nine! Where was the hundredth one?

He counted them again. Yes, one was lost. It must be out on the hills, in the dark, afraid of the hungry wolves that came at night.

The shepherd shut the ninety-nine sheep safely into the

fold. He was tired and hungry, but he could not eat or rest until he had found the lost sheep. He must find it before the wolves came.

'It is true I have ninety-nine sheep that are safely in the fold, but I cannot let the little lost one stay out on the hills, lonely and afraid,' said the good shepherd. So, wrapping his cloak around him, for the wind was cold, and taking a lantern in his hand, he set off in the darkness.

The lost sheep was far away, hiding in a hollow under a bush. It was frightened and lonely. It had wandered away from the flock that day, and had not found them again. When night came, it had listened for the shepherd's call, but it was too far away to hear it. It had wandered farther and farther, and now, afraid of the fierce wolves, it was trembling in the darkness.

The shepherd went all over the hills, calling for his lost sheep. He stumbled over the rough places, and his cloak was caught by brambles. Where was the lost sheep? Surely he was not too late? The wolves would not yet have found it?

The shepherd looked for hours, and then, quite suddenly, he came upon the trembling sheep, hidden under the bush. He knelt down by it to make sure it was not hurt. It was young and small, not much more than a lamb. It nuzzled against the good shepherd, glad to see him again and hear his voice.

'Come with me,' said the shepherd. 'I will carry you back to the fold, little one. How glad I am to find you!'

So the shepherd carried the sheep all the way home, and when he got back, he called to his friends in joy. 'See, I have found my sheep that was lost! Rejoice with me!'

Prayer

Jesus, loving Shepherd, I am one of your lambs. If, when you count your sheep, there comes a day when I am lost, I pray you look for me and find me. I am lost when I do wrong, I wander away from you when I am selfish and unkind. Do not leave me in the darkness, but seek for me and carry me back to the fold. I am one of your lambs. Guard me and keep me, loving Shepherd, all the days of my life.

Amen

The boy with the loaves and fishes

(John vi. 2–14)

There was once a small boy who went fishing. He caught two small fishes and ran home to show them to his mother.

'I will pickle them for you,' she said. 'You shall have them tomorrow.'

Now, when the next day came, the little boy looked out from his house in the hills and saw a great crowd of people in the country roads that ran round the big lake where he had caught his fish.

'Look, Mother!' he cried. 'Why are there so many people there? I shall go and see.'

Soon he was back again. 'There is a wonderful man called Jesus coming, and the people are following him because he does great things. He cures people who are ill. He even makes dead people come alive again. Mother, let me go and see him, please!'

'Very well, you may go,' said his mother. 'But wait a minute – take something to eat with you. Look, here are your two small pickled fish, and five little loaves as well. I'll put them into a basket for you.'

The boy ran off with his basket. Soon he came to the

crowds of people, and he made his way through them until he came to Jesus. He stood and gazed at the kind, loving face of the man sitting on a rock, telling some of his wonderful stories to the listening people.

All day long the people listened to Jesus, and the little boy listened too. He forgot about his basket of food.

But, when the evening came, and Jesus saw that the people were hungry and tired, he was sad. He sent his disciples through the crowd to see if there was any food. The little boy heard them asking the same question as they went here and there.

'Has anyone any food to spare?'

The little boy suddenly remembered his basket of loaves and fishes. He went timidly up to the nearest disciple and touched his arm. 'I have this,' he said, holding up his basket.

The disciple took the boy to Jesus. 'Master,' he said, 'there is a lad here with five small loaves and two fishes.'

Jesus smiled at the boy and took the little basket. 'Thank you,' he said. 'It is just what I need.'

Then he made all the people sit down in little groups, and he took the loaves from the basket, looked up to heaven and blessed the bread. He divided the little fishes up too, and called to his disciples to fetch the food. They came up one by one, and to the little boy's great surprise there was enough for the disciples to take to everyone in the great crowd sitting so patiently on the hillside.

The small boy had some too, and he sat there, his eyes shining, thinking of how he had caught the fishes that everyone was eating, and how his mother had baked the bread.

'I gave them to Jesus and he took them and did a miracle

with them,' he kept thinking. 'Oh – what will Mother say when she hears this wonderful thing! It's the greatest day of my life!'

Prayer

O Lord Jesus, once, long ago, a little boy gave you five barley loaves and two small fishes. You took them and blessed them and you used them to feed hungry people.

What have I to bring you that you will take and bless? I will bring you a loving heart that does kindness to others for your sake. I will bring you loving hands that will do things for others. Take them and bless them and use them as you did the little boy's gift long ago.

Amen

The beggar who shouted

(Luke xviii. 35–43)

One day long ago many beggars sat by a busy roadside. People passed to and fro, and the beggars called to them for bread or money.

One of the beggars was blind. His name was Bartimaeus, and he could not do any work because he could not see. He could only sit by the wayside and cry out to the passers-by.

One morning he sat there in the hot sun, listening to the footfalls of the people passing to and fro. It seemed to him as if there were many more than usual. It sounded as if crowds of people were hurrying along the road!

'Why are there so many people?' asked Bartimaeus, puzzled. 'Tell me, somebody. I can't see what all the excitement is about.'

'Oh, haven't you heard?' said a nearby beggar. 'Jesus of Nazareth is passing by here. We are watching for him. Surely you have heard of him, Bartimaeus?'

Bartimaeus sat still in surprise and delight. 'Jesus of Nazareth! To think he should be coming down this road! He will pass by me. Jesus of Nazareth! He is the great and wonderful healer. How can I make him see me? Oh, somehow I must make him see me!'

After a while the crowds in the road became noisy and excited. Jesus was coming near! Nobody bothered about Bartimaeus or even answered his questions. He couldn't see if it was really Jesus who was coming near, because of his blindness. How could he find out?

Then Bartimaeus lifted up his voice and began to shout loudly, 'Jesus, have pity on me! Jesus, have mercy on me!'

'Be quiet!' said everyone nearby. 'How dare a beggar like you make such a noise?'

But Bartimaeus could not be stopped. He shouted more loudly than he had ever shouted in his life.

'Jesus! Jesus, have mercy on me!'

People came and scolded him. 'Be quiet! You don't suppose that Jesus wants to hear *your* voice, do you?'

'Jesus, have pity on me!' shouted Bartimaeus.

And then Jesus heard that anxious, desperate voice. He stopped and saw the blind man sitting by the wayside.

'Bring him here to me,' he commanded. Then people ran to Bartimaeus and helped him up quickly.

'Now cheer up, Bartimaeus,' they said. 'Jesus is calling for you.'

Bartimaeus flung away his cloak, stretched out his hands, and tried to feel his way to Jesus. The people guided him gently.

Jesus looked at the blind beggar with pity. 'What do you want me to do for you?' he asked.

'O Lord, if only I might see!' said Bartimaeus.

'You shall see!' said Jesus – and Bartimaeus suddenly found himself in light and sunshine, instead of in the darkness he was used to. He could see!

He could see Jesus of Nazareth, the man he had waited for. He could follow him, singing and shouting. There was no man more joyful that day than Bartimaeus, who had once been a poor blind beggar.

Prayer

Dear Lord Jesus, I want to remember tonight those who are blind and cannot see, and those who are ill and in pain.

You are no longer here in this world to put your hands on people who are blind or ill or sad, but I pray to you in heaven to comfort all who need it. Let me do what I can too, for I am here in the world. I can help the blind, and visit the sick and give to the poor.

You always heard when unhappy people called out to you, as Bartimaeus did long ago. Let me hear them too, and stop to help just as you did.

Amen

The little man who climbed the tree

(*Luke xix. 1–10*)

In the big town of Jericho there was a man that nobody liked. His name was Zacchaeus, and he was a collector of taxes.

'We do not like him because he takes more money from us than he should,' said the people. 'He is a dishonest fellow.'

Sometimes this made Zacchaeus sad, because although in many ways he was not a good man, he was not altogether bad. There was some goodness in his heart, hidden away, waiting to grow.

Now one day Zacchaeus heard that the great preacher, Jesus, was coming to Jericho. 'I really must see him,' thought Zacchaeus. 'I have heard such wonderful tales about him.'

So he went to join the crowds that were in the streets to welcome Jesus. But because he was so short Zacchaeus could not see anything at all except the shoulders of the people in front of him.

He tried to get to the front, but as soon as people saw that it was Zacchaeus, the man they so much disliked, they pushed him back. 'Don't let Zacchaeus get to the front,' they said. 'Keep him back.'

Then Zacchaeus had a bright idea. 'I will climb that big

tree whose branches overhang the road!' he said. 'Then I will have a fine view!'

So he quickly climbed the tree and slid along the wide branch. Now he could see everything! And there was Jesus, coming along the road. Zacchaeus feasted his eyes on him. What a noble face! What a gracious smile! What kind, understanding eyes! Zacchaeus loved Jesus, as he lay there on the branch of the tree.

Then suddenly he had the greatest surprise of his life! Jesus looked up at him. He spoke to Zacchaeus.

'Zacchaeus! Make haste and come down because today I must come to your house.'

Zacchaeus slid down the tree. He ran home. He prepared the best meal he could, and made Jesus welcome. But, as Jesus sat at the meal, angry people looked in at the door. Zacchaeus could quite well hear what they were saying about him.

'If Jesus knew what *we* know about that dishonest fellow, he would not eat with him!'

Zacchaeus was ashamed that Jesus should hear so many bad things about him. He looked at Jesus to see if he had heard. Yes, he had. Jesus looked back at Zacchaeus, sadness and kindness in his eyes. 'Oh Zacchaeus, Zacchaeus,' he seemed to say, 'you have goodness in your heart, and yet you have done so much wrong!'

And then Zacchaeus knew that he must put things right at once. He stood up and spoke loudly so that everyone could hear.

'Behold, Master! I shall give half my goods to the poor! And if I have ever robbed a man I will give it back to him four times over!'

'You are one of God's children, Zacchaeus,' said Jesus, very happy to know that because he had seen the secret goodness in Zacchaeus's heart, he had been able to make it grow.

And Zacchaeus was happy too. He had found someone who believed in him, and would help him to be good.

Prayer

Dear Lord Jesus, look into my heart, as you looked into the heart of Zacchaeus, and see what is hidden there.

You will find goodness and badness, kindness and unkindness, truthfulness and untruthfulness, good temper and bad temper.

Come to me as you came to Zacchaeus, let me honour you and love you. Then the bad things in my heart will wither away and the good things will grow, and you will tell me that I, like Zacchaeus, am one of God's children.

Amen

A nobleman goes to Jesus

(John iv. 43–54)

There was once a nobleman who lived in Capernaum by the Lake of Galilee. He had a little son who was all the world to him. One day the child fell ill. His head was hot, his eyes were too bright, and he could not eat.

The nobleman sent a servant to fetch the doctor. But when he came he said at once that the child was too ill to get better.

'I will send for another doctor. I will send for every doctor in Capernaum!' said the nobleman, for he was rich and did not mind how much he spent. So many doctors came, but not one of them could do anything for the little boy.

Then one of his servants spoke to him. 'Sir! There is a wonderful healer called Jesus. He can make sick people well. Shall I go and ask him to come here?'

'Where is this doctor?' asked the nobleman. '*I* will go to him myself. I will beg him to come here to my poor little son.'

'He is at Cana, sir,' said the servant. 'I will send for your horse at once.'

The nobleman set off. Who was this Jesus? He asked those he met, and they told him that Jesus was not a doctor, but someone who could do marvellous things because of the love in his heart.

The nobleman at last came to the house where Jesus was. As soon as the nobleman came into the room he knew that here was the only one in the world who could help him. 'Sir!' he said, 'my little boy is dying in Capernaum. I know you can make him well again. I pray you come back with me to the little son I love so much.'

Jesus looked at the man, and said, 'You and others want to see me do miracles,' he said. 'You will not believe me unless I do these things.'

'Sir, I have not come to see signs and wonders,' said the nobleman. 'All I want is to ask you please to come home with me before my little son dies.'

Then Jesus was filled with pity for the anxious man. 'Go home,' he said. 'Your son lives.'

The nobleman believed Jesus at once and his heart was filled with joy. He hurried away, quite sure that Jesus had spoken the truth. Jesus had not seen the little boy or spoken to him, but in some way the great power of his love had reached out to the child and made him well.

When the man came near his home, he saw that his servants were looking for him with joyful faces. 'Sir!' they called, running to meet him, 'your son is well! See, here he is!'

The little boy came out to leap into his father's arms. The nobleman pressed him close, tears of joy in his eyes. 'When did he get better?' he asked his servants.

'Sir, it was at seven o'clock,' said the servants.

'It was at seven that Jesus said my son would live,' said the nobleman, in awe and wonder. And from that day the nobleman and all his household believed the things that Jesus preached, and praised his name.

Prayer

O Lord Jesus, many people thanked you when you were on earth for the things you did for them. You did many wonders, you told the children stories, you tried to make everyone happy.

Let me too thank you for all you have done for me. Thank you for those who love me and for my mother and father, and teach me to love them. Thank you for my home and for my toys, and for all the things I love.

Amen

The eleventh day

The woman at the dinner party

(Luke vii. 36–50)

There was once a rich man who thought he would ask Jesus to have dinner with him.

'Jesus is only a poor preacher,' thought the man, who was called Simon. 'I shall not bother to make any fuss over him. It's an honour for him to be asked to a house as grand as mine!'

So, when Jesus came, Simon did not send a servant to meet him with a jug and bowl of water to wash his tired dusty feet, as was the custom in that country. Simon did not even come to greet him.

Jesus saw all this but he said nothing. He took his place at the table and began to talk in his usual interesting way.

Now a woman had watched Jesus go into the house. Her name was Mary of Magdalene, and she had been a bad woman who had done wrong things. But she had seen and heard Jesus, and his great goodness had touched her heart and made her sad and ashamed.

'I wish I had not done so many wrong things,' she thought. 'I am not worthy even to look on Jesus. If he knew how ashamed I am, he would be sorry for me, and say something kind.'

45

Mary saw that no servant washed his tired feet or poured oil on his weary head. Simon did not come to greet him. Mary of Magdalene was surprised and sorry. Why did not this rich man do Jesus honour, and give him a great welcome! What a shameful thing!

Mary could not bear that this beloved Jesus should be so poorly treated. She went to a shop in the town and bought a jar of expensive, sweet-smelling ointment, the best they had. It cost a great deal of money but Mary did not mind. Only the best was good enough for Jesus.

She slipped into the house, went to Jesus and kissed his dusty feet. She was so sad and ashamed of her bad life that she wept bitterly, and her tears washed the feet of Jesus. Mary wiped them with her long hair. Then she opened the jar of sweet-smelling ointment to put on his feet.

But she did not rub on only a little. She poured all of it over his feet at once. She felt that she had to give him every-thing.

Now Simon did not like this bad woman coming into his house, and he was shocked that Jesus should allow her to wash his feet. Jesus saw what he was thinking and spoke to him.

'Do you see this woman, Simon? I came into your house, and you gave me no water for my feet; but she has washed my feet with her tears, and wiped them with her hair. You gave me no kiss; but this woman has not stopped kissing my feet since she came in. You did not anoint my head with oil, but this woman has poured oil on my feet.

'And so I say unto her, that her sins, which are many, are forgiven, because she loved so much.' Then Jesus turned to the woman and said, 'Your sins are forgiven. Because of your great love and trust in me, you can be good. Go away and be happy.'

So Mary went away happy, and after that she followed Jesus and did all she could to help him.

Prayer

Dear Lord Jesus, if you came to my house I would do all I could to make you welcome and do you honour. I would give you a present of the things I liked best. I would tell you that it was the greatest day of my life.

But you cannot come to my house now, as you came to Simon's, so I will make you welcome in my heart and do you honour there. I will kneel before you each night and tell you that I am your loving servant. Tell me what you want me to do for you and I will do it.

Amen

The twelfth day

The baby in the bulrushes

(Exodus ii. 3–10)

Long, long ago, before Jesus came, Pharaoh the king ruled over Egypt. When he looked out over his kingdom he saw that there were people there, called Hebrews, who were becoming powerful.

'I must stop these Hebrews from getting so much power,' said Pharaoh, and he thought of a very cruel thing to do. 'Take all the boy babies away from their mothers,' he commanded his soldiers. 'Throw them into the River Nile to drown. Then fewer Hebrew boys will grow up to be strong men.'

When the poor mothers heard this they were filled with fear and great sorrow.

One mother, called Jochabed, had a beautiful baby. 'I cannot let him be thrown into the river!' she said. 'I shall hide him!'

So she hid him for some months. But the baby had such a loud cry that she was afraid the servants of Pharaoh would hear him. What was she to do?

She called her daughter Miriam to her. 'We will make a little ark of bulrushes,' she said. 'We will line it softly for our baby, and put the little ark among the rushes that grow near the pool where Pharaoh's daughter, the princess, bathes every day.'

So Miriam and her mother made a little ark of bulrushes

48

for their baby boy. They plaited the rushes together tightly. They made a lid too, so that they might close it down to shelter him from the sun. They stopped up every crack with pitch and mud, and set the ark in the sun to dry.

Then they lined it with soft blankets and put the baby inside. He soon fell asleep. Then Miriam and her mother took the baby down to the pool where the princess bathed each day.

They hid the ark in some rushes. It floated very well indeed. They whispered good-bye to the sleeping baby and then Jochabed went home. But she left Miriam behind to watch.

Soon Pharaoh's daughter came down to bathe, with her servants round her. She saw the queer little ark floating on the water.

'Go and fetch me that basket,' said the princess. 'I will see what is inside it.'

The maid fetched the basket. It was heavy. She took it to the princess, who opened the lid. Inside was the baby boy! He awoke, and began to cry for his mother.

The princess took him out of the basket and held him lovingly against her. He stopped crying and looked up at her.

'He is beautiful,' said the princess. 'He must be one of the Hebrew babies. I cannot bear him to be killed. I wish he were mine!'

Then Miriam came up timidly. 'Shall I get you a nurse for the child?' she asked, trembling at her daring. The princess smiled and nodded.

So Miriam sped away to fetch her mother and soon Jochabed was with the princess.

49

'Take this child away,' said the princess to Jochabed. 'You shall be his nurse and I will pay you. He shall come to live in my palace when he is old enough.'

Then thankfully Jochabed and Miriam took their baby boy home again, safe and sound. 'Now praise be to God!' said his mother. 'He will not be thrown into the river! He can live at home with us and be happy, until the day comes when he must go to the great palace.'

Prayer

O Lord God, who looked down and saw the baby Moses asleep in his little ark of bulrushes, look down on me too and keep me from all harm. I know that if even a sparrow falls, you see it. Then watch over me, I pray you, and keep those I love from harm and danger too.

Guard me from all evil things; guard my eyes from looking on what I know is wrong; guard my tongue from speaking unkind words; guard my ears from listening to spiteful tales; and guard my mind from every wrong or foolish thought.

Amen

The thirteenth day

The poor woman in the Temple
(Luke xxi. 1–4)

There was once a poor widow who lived in Jerusalem. She had to work very hard because her husband was dead, and she had no one to bring her money to buy food.

She was very, very poor. Her clothes were old and so thin that it was hard even to darn them. She had very little to eat, and hardly any pleasures. She came to pray in the Temple as often as she could. She loved the beautiful House of God, and liked to stand in a corner, saying her prayers in peace.

When Festival Week came the widow went to the Temple as usual to pray. Hundreds of people came to visit Jerusalem that week, and all of them went to pray in the Temple at some time or other. The widow found the courts crowded with strangers who had come to worship and pray.

There were money boxes in the court of the Temple. The Church collected money for all kinds of things, and everyone was supposed to give what he could. The boxes or chests had a trumpet-like opening, and the money was slipped into this and then fell down into the box. All day long people put in money, as they came and went.

Anyone could put in what he liked, but nobody was allowed to put in less than a penny. We have no coin less than half a penny, but in that far-off country there were not only half-pennies, but even quarter-pennies.

The widow woman knew that she must not put in less than a penny. She looked round her and saw everyone putting in much more money than that.

A rich man nearby put in a great deal all at once. Another man slipped in a large sum, enough to feed the widow for a year. Others put in what they could spare, and turned to go.

Now all that the widow had was two mites, which together made a half-penny. She was ashamed to put in such a small sum, and yet it was all she had in the world. So she went to a box in a corner, and slipped in the two mites, hoping that nobody would see how little she had put in.

But somebody did see. Jesus was there with his disciples, watching the people come in and out of the Temple. He had seen the poor widow woman as soon as she had come in, and had thought that surely she could not spare even half a penny. Then he saw her put in the two mites.

'Do you see that poor widow?' he said to his disciples. 'I have watched the rich men putting in great sums of money, but that woman put in only two mites. And yet she has put in more, much more, than anyone else in the Temple. They put in only what they had to spare. She put in everything she had.

'And so, in the eyes of God, her two mites are worth more than all the money the rich men have put in together!'

Prayer

Dear Lord Jesus, who saw the poor widow putting in her mites, help me to be generous in all I do. Let me always give the most I can if there is someone that needs my help.

Let me have an open heart and an open hand, ready to give generously to all who need it, and let me give cheerfully, for the Lord loves a cheerful giver.

Amen

The man who was robbed

(Luke x. 25–37)

Now once there was a man who had to go from Jerusalem to Jericho. He took the lonely mountain road, and travelled alone.

There were robbers hiding in the mountains, and when they saw the traveller coming they lay in wait for him. They pounced on him and caught him. They took off all his clothes, stole the goods he carried, struck him many blows, and then went away.

The poor man was left lying by the roadside, badly hurt. He called for help but nobody was there.

Then he heard the sound of footsteps and he was glad. He lifted his poor head and saw a priest coming, a man of God, who had been to help in the church at Jerusalem. He called to him.

But the priest crossed over to the other side, and would not even look to see why the man cried out. The poor wounded man groaned in despair. But soon he could hear other footsteps.

This time he saw a Levite, a man who worshipped God,

and liked to help in the church. He would help, he would be kind.

The Levite went over to the wounded man. He saw that his clothes and goods had been stolen and that he was badly wounded. He looked at him and then, without a word of comfort, he went on his way. The poor traveller was left alone once more.

Then there came a man on a little donkey. The wounded traveller saw that he was a man of Samaria, a Samaritan, and he sighed. 'Everyone knows that the Samaritans are bad people. Why, the priests and the Levites will not even sleep in the same house with a wicked Samaritan! I can expect no help from him.'

But the Samaritan quickly got off his donkey and went to the wounded man. 'Poor, poor fellow,' he said, leaning over him. 'You have been beaten and robbed. Lie still and I will help you.'

He rubbed the man's wounds with oil and wine. Then he bound them up with strips of cloth. 'I will help you to get on to my donkey,' said the Samaritan. 'You shall ride him to the nearest inn.'

When they came to the inn the Samaritan went to the inn-keeper. 'I want a room for this poor fellow,' he said. 'He is ill and has been robbed. I will take care of him tonight, and to-morrow I will leave him in your care till he is better.'

So he cared for the man that night, and the next day, when he left, he gave the innkeeper some money. 'Take care of him for me,' he said. 'If you spend more money than I have given you, I will pay it to you next time I come.'

Then he said good-bye to the wounded man and went.

Jesus told this story so that people might know what it is to be a good friend. At the end he asked this question:

'Which of the three, the priest, the Levite and the Samaritan, was a good friend to the man who fell among thieves?'

Prayer

Jesus, friend of all the world, help me to be a good friend too. Let me give to those who have less than I have, let me help those who are ill or sad.

You have said that we must love our neighbours as we love ourselves, we must be kind to all who need our kindness. When I am ill I am glad to be cared for and loved, when I am sad I like to be comforted. Then let me do the same for others, and be a good friend to all I meet.

Amen

The fifteenth day

When bread rained from heaven

(Exodus xvi. 1–4, 13–18; xvii. 1–6)

Once there were a great many people travelling together to go to a beautiful land that God had promised to give them.

Their leader was a great man called Moses. You heard of him before when he was a baby hidden in the bulrushes. Do you remember?

There came a time when the people could find no food to eat. Their children came running to them, crying with hunger. 'Give us bread! Why is there no food?'

Then the people grumbled to Moses. 'Why have you brought us here to die of hunger?'

Now God heard the hungry people, and he spoke to Moses. 'Behold,' he said, 'I will rain bread from heaven for you.'

Now, in the morning, the dew fell, as it always did. When the sun rose and shone down warmly the dew dried – and something was left behind!

All over the ground were little round things, as small as hailstones. The children ran to them and picked them up. 'What is it?' they cried.

'This is manna, bread rained from heaven by God,' said Moses. 'Gather it before the sun grows hot. See how the Lord God cares for his hungry people!'

Everyone went to gather up the manna. It tasted like wafers made with honey, and the people liked it very much.

Another day came when, in their travels, the people stayed in a place where there was no water to drink. Thirsty and miserable, they went to Moses.

'We shall die of thirst! Give us water to drink! See how thirsty our poor children are!'

Then Moses went to God again and prayed to him. 'What shall I do with my people? They are so angry because there is no water that they are almost ready to stone me.'

Then the Lord God answered Moses and said, 'Go on in front of the people, and take your staff in your hand. You will come to a great rock. Strike the rock with your staff and I will make water gush forth from it.'

Moses gave thanks to the Lord, and he went in front of the people to find the great rock. He took his staff with him as God had commanded.

After a time he came to a place called Horeb. There he saw the great rock that God had told him about.

He struck the rock with his staff, and behold, water gushed out of it in a great spring. It splashed round about Moses's feet, shining in the sun.

Then the people came gladly to drink, bringing their cups and dishes. Once more God had taken care of them and their children. They sang his praises as they drank the cool water.

'He feeds us with manna from heaven, and he gives us water to drink from a rock. Now praise be to the Lord!'

Prayer

O Lord God, who long ago fed Moses and his hungry people, and cared for them in their journey, look down on all those who are hungry and cold and unhappy tonight, and care for them too.

If there are any children who are hungry and miserable to-night, send them food and comfort. Send them friends who will help them. If I can help too, show me how, and I will do my best.

Thank you for the good food I have, the cosy bed, the warm clothes, and for all the happiness I have here in my home.

Amen

The sixteenth day

A man who went out to sow
(*Luke viii. 5–15*)

Once upon a time a man went out to sow seed in his field. He wanted to see strong grain growing there so that he might reap it and make good bread for his family.

He scattered the seed by hand, throwing it first this side and then that.

There was a path nearby, trodden hard by the people who used it. Some of the seeds fell on this hard ground. The birds saw them easily and came down to peck them up. So those seeds could not grow.

Some of the ground in the field was very stony. The seeds that fell there had very little earth to grow in. Still, they put out tiny roots and little green shoots.

But when the sun shone down hotly the little plants were scorched; they had not enough earth to grow deep roots, and they withered away.

Some of the seeds fell among thick weeds. They too put out roots and shoots, but when they grew, the weeds grew too, and they were choked, because they had not enough light and air. So they died.

But many seeds fell on good ground, where there were no

stones or weeds. They grew up tall and sturdy and became a waving field of grain.

When the farmer came he looked in delight at his field. 'My seeds have given me thirty, sixty, or maybe a hundred times as much grain as I sowed!' he said. 'I am proud of my harvest.'

Now this was a story that Jesus told to the listening people. His twelve friends listened too, and they asked him what his story meant.

'I will tell you,' said Jesus. 'The words of God, our Father in Heaven, go out all over the world. We read his word in our Bible, we hear it told us by many good people. God's word is like the seed in my story, scattered everywhere.

'But there are some people who will not hear God's word. They take no notice, so that the seed falls on hard ground and will not grow.

'Other people listen for a little while, but soon give up. They are like the stony ground, where the seeds only grew for a short time and then died.

'Then there are people whose hearts are bad, and who are choked with wrong thoughts. They are like the weedy ground, where good seed could not grow because the weeds choked it.

'But there are many others who listen to God's word, and store it away in their hearts, letting it grow there into goodness and kindness. They are the people we love the most, because their lives are full of loving kindness. They are the good ground, where the seed gives thirty, sixty or even a hundred times more than was sown.'

Prayer

O Lord Jesus, I have heard your words tonight, I have listened to the story you told. Your words are the good seed that must fall on good ground. I will not be the hard ground where the seeds are pecked by birds; I will not be the stony field or the weeds; I want to be the good earth where the seed will grow and bring forth a wonderful harvest. Help me, Lord, to listen and remember, and to bring forth a harvest you will be glad to reap.

Amen

The seventeenth day

A little boat in a storm

(Mark iv. 35–41)

One evening Jesus felt tired. He had been telling the people stories all day long, and now he needed a rest.

'We will take the boat to the other side of the lake,' he said to Peter and the other disciples. 'Then nobody can follow us.'

So out on the open lake sailed the fishing boat. Peter put a cushion behind Jesus's head. He saw that his Master was very tired.

Jesus lay down in the boat and closed his eyes. He felt the waves lifting the boat up and down, he heard the splashing of the water. He was so tired that he fell sound asleep.

'Do not wake him,' said Peter. 'Let him sleep.'

The little boat went on and on. The darkness began to fall, and the waters of the lake grew purple. Then Peter pointed out something that made him afraid.

'See,' he said, looking up into the darkening sky. 'See! A great black cloud is blowing over the hills. The wind is rising quickly! A storm is coming!'

The other disciples looked up at the great cloud. They knew what sharp, sudden storms sometimes blew down on the lake. When that happened the waves rose high, the wind roared, and any boats on the water were in great danger.

Darkness came down. The wind suddenly roared round the boat, which rocked to and fro on the rising waves. Spray blew over the fishermen in the boat, and they peered anxiously into the darkness.

'Shall we reach the other side in safety?' they said to one another.

'Look! The waves are splashing right into our boat!' said Peter, in alarm. 'It will fill with water. It will sink and we shall be drowned.'

Jesus did not wake, even when the waves splashed over him. Peter shook him by the shoulder, and shouted in his ear, and the others shouted too.

'Master, Master, we shall be drowned. Save us!'

Jesus awoke. He looked round into the darkness, heard the roaring wind and felt the foam from the angry waves. He stood up in the swaying boat.

'Peace, be still,' he said to the storm.

All at once the wind sank down to a whisper, and the waves no longer rocked the boat, for there came a great calm over the lake. Jesus turned to his disciples, who were so frightened and amazed that they could not say a word.

'Why are you so afraid?' asked Jesus. 'Could you not trust me?'

Then the disciples were filled with wonder. 'What kind of man is this?' they said to one another. 'Even the wind and the waves bow down before him!'

Prayer

Dear Lord Jesus, I would have been afraid too when the storm came down on the lake, and the boat was filled with water. I would have wanted to waken you and cry for help.

I know that if I ask your help you will always give it to me. If I am afraid you will make me brave. If I am not strong enough to face danger or difficulty and I cry out to you, you will always help me, as you helped your disciples long ago.

Be with me always, dear Lord Jesus, and I will be brave and strong.

Amen

The little girl who slept

(Mark v. 21–24, 35–43)

There was once a little girl who lived in the town of Capernaum, by the blue lake of Galilee.

Her father Jairus loved her very much, because she was his only child. He played with her and brought her presents, and they were very happy together.

One day she fell ill. She would not eat and she would not smile. Her mother felt her hot head and looked anxiously at Jairus. 'She is very ill. You must ask the doctor to come.'

So the doctor came, but he could not make the little girl better. Other doctors came, but they all shook their heads. 'We can do nothing. Your little girl is very ill. She will die.'

'Oh no, no!' said poor Jairus. 'Is there nothing we can do?'

Then he remembered hearing of a man called Jesus. He spoke to his weeping wife. 'Wife, shall I go and ask Jesus to come? Perhaps he can do something for our little girl.'

'Yes, go. Go now,' said his wife, and Jairus went quickly out of the house and into the town. 'Do you know where Jesus is?' he asked everyone he met. And at last someone did know.

'Yes. He has gone over the lake in a boat. He may be back soon.'

Jairus went down to the lakeside to wait. He looked anxiously over the water. Was there a boat coming? If Jesus was gone a long time it might be too late.

Then a cry went up. 'Here comes the boat! Jesus is coming!'

As soon as the boat touched the shore Jairus knelt down before Jesus. 'I pray you, Sir, come to my little daughter,' he begged. 'She is at the point of death; but if you will lay your hands on her she will live.'

Jesus saw how troubled the poor man was and he went with him at once. When they were near Jairus's house, messengers came out. 'Do not trouble Jesus,' said one of them. 'Your little girl is dead.'

Tears ran down Jairus's face. Jesus spoke gently to him. 'Do not be afraid; only believe.' Then they went to the house, and Jesus told the crowd behind him that they must not come any farther. He went in with Peter and John and Jairus.

The house was full of people wailing and crying. 'Why do you make this noise?' said Jesus. 'The little girl is not dead, only asleep.'

But they laughed at him in scorn. Then Jesus went into the room where the little girl lay, still and white on her small bed. Her mother stood weeping beside her.

Jesus took the child's hand in his. 'Little maid,' he said, 'I say unto you, arise!'

And the little girl sat up, looking round her, astonished to see her mother and father weeping. She got out of bed and walked.

71

Crying for joy, her mother took her into her arms, and Jairus stroked her curls. It was the happiest day of his life. He had gone to Jesus in sadness, and, because he had believed, his little girl was well again, and he was happy.

Prayer

Great Lord Jesus, who cares for little children and their fathers and mothers, watch over me and my family, and guard us from all evil. If sadness comes I will go to look for you as Jairus did, and pray you to help me. I cannot go to the lake to wait for you, but I can kneel by my bed and pray. If I am afraid or sad or ashamed I will come to find you, and I shall know that you will be with me to comfort me and help.

Amen

The voice in the night

(*1 Samuel i. 9–28; iii. 1–10*)

Once there was a woman called Hannah who was very sad because she had no children. She went to the Temple of God and stood there, praying, with tears running down her cheeks.

'O Lord God, I pray you to give me a little son of my own,' begged Hannah. 'Let me have a baby boy, and when he grows I will give him back to you, to serve you in your church.'

Now Eli, the old priest of the Temple, heard her praying. 'Go in peace,' he said. 'May the Lord God grant you your wish.'

Hannah's wish was granted, and she was overjoyed when she at last had a little baby son to sit on her knee. She knew that she must keep her promise to God when he was old enough – but until then he was her very own to love and care for.

The day came when she must take him to Eli in the Temple. She was sad to say good-bye to the beautiful child. 'I will come each year to see you,' she said, 'and I will bring you a new coat each time. See, my lord Eli, I have kept my promise to God, and I have given my son to him to serve him. May he grow up to be a great and good man!'

Then she left him. Samuel felt lonely at first, but he soon

grew to love the Temple and the work he had to do. He was dressed like a little priest in white linen with an embroidered belt. He soon learned all the things he had to do in the Temple, and he learned too about God and his commandments. Each year his mother came to see him, bringing him a new coat she had made.

Now God looked down on his Temple and saw Samuel and loved him. Here was someone who would work for him, and who would show the people how to be good. So he called to Samuel in the middle of the night, as the boy lay sleeping.

'Samuel!'

Samuel awoke at once. He thought it was Eli calling him and he went to him. 'Here I am. You called me.'

'No, I did not call you,' said Eli. 'Lie down again.'

When Samuel was lying down he heard the voice again. 'Samuel!' So again he got up and went to Eli, saying, 'Here am I, for truly you called me!'

'No, I did not call you, my son,' said Eli. 'Lie down again.'

Then a third time the voice called Samuel and he ran to Eli, and this time Eli knew that it must be God's voice speaking to the boy.

'Go lie down,' said Eli, 'and if the Lord calls you again, say "Speak, Lord, for your servant hears you".'

Then, a little afraid, Samuel went to lie down once more, and again he heard the voice saying, 'Samuel, Samuel!'

And Samuel answered at once. 'Speak, Lord, for your servant hears you.' And then God spoke to Samuel and told him many things. He told him what he must do, and Samuel listened in awe and wonder.

Samuel grew up to be a great man and a great preacher – but even when he was an old man he never forgot the night that God came to him and called him for the very first time.

Prayer

Lord God, who spoke to the boy Samuel in the middle of the night, speak to me too. Call me if you want work done that I can do. I shall know in my heart when you need me to do something, and I will do it, even though it may be hard.

I will listen always for your voice, and when I hear you calling me, in the middle of my work or play, I will answer at once, as Samuel did, 'Speak, Lord, for your servant hears you.'

Amen

The twentieth day

A den of thieves

(Luke xix. 45–48)

There was a time when Jesus was very angry.

He went to Jerusalem to go to the Temple, the beautiful church there, to pray to God his Father in Heaven. He came into the outer courts of the Temple, and stood looking round in anger and disgust.

'It is nothing but a market!' said Jesus. 'See how people buy and sell here, look at all the animals fastened up, see how dirty and noisy the House of God is!'

And indeed it was. Oxen, sheep, doves, and goats were being bought and sold. People were changing their money there, and many of them were being cheated by the money-changers. Boys and girls ran through the courts, taking a short cut there to save time.

The beautiful courts smelled badly and were noisy and full of dirt. The frightened sheep bleated and the oxen lowed. People shouted across to one another. Who would think that this was a Temple, the House of God, a place in which to pray and worship?

Jesus looked round and knew that he must stop the people treating the church in that way. He was full of anger and sadness.

He shouted to the people to leave the Temple courts and go away. He went to the tables where people were changing their money, and upset them. The money began to roll here and there, and the people dived after it.

Then Jesus overturned the stalls where people were buying and selling, and drove away those who were using the courts as a short cut.

Soon there was a great commotion. 'What is happening? What is this man doing? Why is he upsetting the tables and the stalls?'

'Pick up our money! Stop this man from overturning the tables! Who is he and why does he do this?'

Then Jesus, alone and unafraid among the angry crowd, answered them sternly: 'In the Bible it is written that God's House shall be a House of Prayer. But you have made it into a den of thieves!'

Nobody dared to shout against Jesus or to strike him. 'We will go to the Chief Priests and complain,' said the angry money-changers and sellers of animals.

But the ordinary people were glad to see someone so fearless as Jesus, for they knew that he was right. They gathered round him, eager to hear him preach in the Temple.

The children who had seen him turning out the men who made the Temple into a market came along to him and cheered him. 'Hosanna to the Son of David!' they cried. And they crowded round him to hear him tell his stories.

The Chief Priests could do nothing to stop Jesus preaching in the Temple, because the people loved him so much. So, for a while at least, the House of God was quiet and lovely, as Jesus had meant it to be.

Prayer

O Jesus, brave and fearless, help me to stand up for the right as you did, when you turned the crowds out of the Temple. Do not let me be afraid of what people might say or do to me. Let me never be ashamed of saying and doing what I know is right.

Help me to be brave and fearless always, to speak the truth, to own up when I have done wrong, and to stand up unafraid against anything that is not good and right.

Amen

The boy who went away

(*Luke xv. 11–32*)

There was once a man who had two sons. They lived on their father's big farm, and had plenty of good food to eat and fine clothes to wear.

The elder son worked hard and was happy. The younger one was idle and bored. He did not like the life on the farm. He wanted to go to the gay, busy town and live there. So one day he went to his father and begged him to give him his share of the money, and let him go. The father was sad, but he gave his son his money, and the boy went off gaily.

He came to the far-off town. He bought himself grand clothes, and feasted every day. When the people there saw that he had plenty of money they came round him to share it. He gave great feasts, and kept many servants.

But one day he found that he had no money left – and when his money went, his friends went also. Then there came a great famine in that land, so that there was very little to eat. The young man had to look for work and there was not much that he could find, for he was not used to working hard.

But at last he was given a job. He had to look after a herd of pigs, and feed them on empty pods and husks. Very often the young man would have liked to eat the pigs' food, for he was faint with hunger.

He was very sad. He remembered his father's big farm, and all the servants who had plenty of food to eat, much more then he had.

'I will arise and go to my father,' said the young man. 'I will say to him, "Father, I have done wrong in God's sight and in yours too, and I am no longer worthy to be called your son. Let me be one of your servants."'

So he went back to his father's farm, and, when he was still a good way off, his father, who was always watching for him, saw him and ran to him. He put his arms round his son and kissed him.

Then the young man knelt down before him and said, 'Father, I have done wrong in God's sight and in yours too and I am no longer worthy to be called your son.'

But his father would not let him say any more. He called gladly to his servants. 'Bring out the best clothes we have and put them on my son. Get a ring too, and put it on his finger, and bring shoes for his feet. We will have a great feast to-night. We will eat and be merry, for this son of mine I thought was dead is alive again; he was lost, but now he is found.'

Then fine clothes and shoes were brought and put on the young man. A ring was set on his finger. From the kitchen came the smell of a great feast being prepared.

The young man was so grateful for this wonderful welcome that he could have cried for joy. How could he ever have left his kind, loving father? Ah, how he would work for him now, so that he might earn his forgiveness and show him how much he loved him for his great kindness!

Prayer

Dear Lord Jesus, I love your story of the son who left his father, and came back poor and in rags, and was welcomed gladly by him.

I know that if any of your children leave your Kingdom of Love, and turn their backs on you, you will never forget them, but, like the father in the story, will watch for them to come back again. And when they come back you will welcome them lovingly.

So, dear Lord Jesus, if I ever stray away from you, watch for me till I come back to beg your forgiveness. I shall always know that your love is waiting for me, just as in your story the father waited for his son.   *Amen*

The twenty-second day

The ungrateful servant

(*Matthew xviii. 21–35*)

One day Peter came to Jesus and asked him a question.

'Lord,' he said, 'how often must I forgive my brother if he does wrong to me? Shall I forgive him as much as seven times?' Jesus smiled at Peter's question. 'No, Peter,' he said, 'not seven times – but seventy times seven!' And then he told Peter a story to show him what he meant.

'Once upon a time,' said Jesus, 'there was a great king who had many servants. Some of them owed him money and came to pay it. But one man, who owed him a very large sum, had no money to pay his debt.

' "Then," said the king, "you must sell all your goods to get the money. You must sell your wife and your children too as servants, and you must sell yourself."

'The man was filled with horror and misery. What! Was he to lose his house and all his goods? Was he to take the wife he loved and sell her to someone to work as a slave? Was he to sell his dear children, too, and perhaps never see them again? He would have to sell himself as well, and he would never be happy again.

'He flung himself down before the king. "Sir, great lord and master, forgive me! Be patient for a little while and I will work and pay all the money I owe you. Have mercy on me, lord!"

83

'The king looked down at the unhappy man and was sorry for him. He was a kind and merciful king, who hated to see anyone unhappy.

' "Get up," he said. "I forgive you all you owe me. You shall not sell your goods, your wife or your children. I will forgive you."

'The man went away very happy indeed. He went to his family and they all rejoiced with him. What kindness and mercy the king had shown!

'Now a little while after that, this man met one of his fellow servants, who owed him a small sum of money.

'Did he forgive his fellow servant, and show the same pity that he himself had been shown? No, he did not. Instead he went to him, took him by the throat and shook him roughly.

' "Pay me what you owe me!" he shouted.

'Then the other servant fell down on his knees and begged for mercy. "Forgive me! Be patient for a little while and I will work and pay you all the money I owe you!"

'But the man would not forgive him. He had his fellow servant put into prison, where he was very unhappy.

'Now, when the other servants heard about this they were angry and went to the king to tell him what the first servant had done. The king called the bad servant to him at once and spoke to him sternly:

' "O, you wicked servant, I forgave you everything! Why then did you not forgive your fellow servant and take pity on him, as I took pity on you?"

'And the king was very angry and sent the man to prison to be well punished for his wickedness.'

Prayer

Dear Lord Jesus, forgive me for all the wrong things I do each day. Forgive me for the times when I am angry or selfish, unkind or untruthful. Forgive me when I forget that I belong to your Kingdom of Love, and take me back again.

Help me too to forgive other people. Let me be kind and do as you told Peter to do – forgive those who do wrong or unkind things to me.

Amen

The twenty-third day

The man who came through the roof

(Mark ii. 1–12)

Now there was once a man who was sick, and lay in bed all day long, miserable and ill. He had kind friends who came to see him, but there were many hours when he was quite alone.

In those lonely hours the man wondered why he was ill. 'Perhaps it is a punishment for all the wrong things I have done in my life,' thought the man. 'I am sorry for my sins. I wish they could be forgiven. If I could live my life over again I would do better.'

One day his friends came to him in excitement. 'You know that wonderful healer called Jesus? Well, he is here, in this town!'

'Here – in this town?' said the man on the bed. 'Oh, how I wish I could see him.'

'We will take you to him!' said his friends and they lifted up his mattress by the corners and set off to find Jesus.

Jesus was sitting in a house not far off. It was one of many houses built round a courtyard. When the men with the mattress came to the courtyard it was already crowded with people who wanted to see and hear Jesus.

'We can't get in!' they said in despair. 'We can't even get through the gate! What shall we do? We *must* get our friend to Jesus.'

'I know what we will do,' said one of the men. 'We will go up to the flat roof of the house that Jesus is in, make a hole in it, and then let down our friend by tying ropes to the ends of his mattress!'

'Will you do that for me?' asked the sick man, eagerly. He soon saw that they would, for they got ropes and tied them firmly to each end of his mattress. Then they carried him up the steps to the flat roof. Many roofs were flat in that country, because the people liked to sleep on them in hot weather. Most of them had roofs made of earth.

This roof was made of earth, too. The men began to dig a hole in it! Soon they could see down into the room below.

The hole was made much bigger – big enough to let down the man on his mattress – and down he came, clinging to his mattress, and was laid to rest before Jesus.

The sick man looked up at Jesus, and saw his noble face and kind eyes. Jesus knew at once what the man wanted. He was sorry for all the wrong he had done in his life, and he wanted to be forgiven.

'Man,' said Jesus, 'your sins are forgiven you.'

A great happiness came into the man's heart, which leaped for joy when he heard Jesus say, 'Arise, take up your bed, and go to your house.'

And the man arose, took up his bed, and went out, praising God loudly, so full of amazement and happiness that he hardly knew what he was doing.

And everyone was filled with astonishment and said, 'We have seen strange things this day; yes, we have seen strange and wonderful things!'

Prayer

Dear Lord Jesus, you did many wonderful things when you were here on earth, and I like to hear about them.

If I had been one of the sick people you cured, or the blind people whose eyes you made better, I would have knelt down to thank you for all you had done for me.

I thank you now for my health and strength, for my legs that can run fast, my eyes that can see well, and my hands that can do so many things.

Amen

David and the giant

(*1 Samuel xvii. 20–50*)

Long before Jesus lived in the world, there was a boy called David, who was fearless and brave. He was a shepherd boy, and once he had killed a lion who had come to eat his sheep.

Now his three brothers had gone to join an army that was fighting a fierce enemy, the Philistines. David was sent to take his brothers some bread and cheese, and he wandered through the camp to find them.

Suddenly he heard a tremendous voice shouting from the opposite hill, and he looked there and saw a great giant. He wore a glittering brass helmet on his head, and heavy armour. He had an enormous spear, and before him went a man carrying a great shining shield.

'Choose a man and let him come to fight me!' roared the giant. 'If your man beats me, then I and all the Philistines will be your servants; but if I beat him, then you must be our servants!'

The giant had roared out these words for forty days, and not one man had dared to fight him. David heard the giant and was astonished that no one would go against him.

'Is no one brave enough to kill this giant?' he said. 'I will fight him myself!'

Now when Saul, the king, heard that David had said this, he sent for him and spoke to him. 'You are only a boy. This man is a giant, and has been a soldier for years!'

'The Lord God helped me when a lion came to take my sheep,' said David, 'and he helped me to kill a bear, too. Will he not help me to fight this giant?'

'Go and fight him then, and the Lord go with you,' said Saul the king.

He gave David a heavy helmet of brass to wear, and a great coat of armour for his body. David put his sword by his side, and then tried to walk. But the armour was much too heavy for him.

So he took off the helmet and the armour and laid down the sword. He picked up his staff and went down to the brook. He found five smooth pebbles and put them into his little bag. Then he took his sling and went up the hill to where the enormous Philistine stood.

The giant was astonished to see David, and he laughed and shouted scornfully. David shouted back boldly:

'You come to me with a sword, a spear and a shield, but I come to you in the name of God who will fight with me and conquer you!'

Then David put his hand into his bag and took out a smooth stone. He put it into his sling, whirled it about, and flung the stone straight at the giant.

It hit him on the forehead, where he had no armour, and killed him. The giant fell down on his face and lay still, and all the Philistines cried out in fear, and fled away.

But David, and all Saul's men, shouted for joy, and ran to chase the Philistines and defeat them. And so there was a great victory that day, and much rejoicing.

'We will praise the Lord God, whose hand guided the hand of David!' sang Saul's men. 'There is no one, not even a giant, who can stand against the might of the Lord.'

Prayer

O Lord God, let me be a David too, and fight against giants for you. I know there are not giants now like the one that David killed, but there are others I can fight in your name.

I will fight the giants of selfishness and unkindness, and the giants of untruthfulness and meanness; I will defeat the giants of laziness and deceit, and all the other giants there are.

I will say, as David did, that I come against them in the name of God, who will fight with me and conquer them.

Stand beside me always, Lord God, and I shall never be afraid.
Amen

The twenty-fifth day

Walking on the waves

(Matthew xiv. 22–33)

One evening Jesus wanted to go alone into the hills by the lake and pray.

'Take the boat and go to the other side of the lake,' he told his disciples. 'I will come to you when I am ready.'

So they got into their boat and began to row over the waters. Jesus walked up into the hills and began to pray to his Heavenly Father. He prayed to him for many hours, and then came down to the lake.

The wind was blowing very hard. He could hear the roar of the waves as they broke on the shore. He looked for the boat, and, when the moon came out from behind a cloud, he saw it.

Peter and the others had had a hard time rowing the boat that night. The wind had suddenly come up and had made great waves on the lake. The boat was tossed to and fro, and although the disciples rowed hard they could not seem to go very far.

They began to be afraid, and wished that Jesus was with them. 'If he were here, he would help us,' they said. 'Where is he? Perhaps he is still praying up in the hills. He may not know that a storm has arisen on the lake.'

But Jesus did know. He had been watching the boat toss about on the waves, and he knew how difficult it was for the disciples to row to safety. He knew too that they were wishing he was with them.

'I will go to them and help them,' thought Jesus. Then he did a strange and wonderful thing.

He walked over the waves to the boat. When he was near to them the disciples caught sight of his white figure on the tossing waves.

Then they heard the voice of Jesus coming over the water to them. 'Be of good cheer! It is I; be not afraid.'

His voice sounded clearly over the roar of the wind and waves. The disciples were amazed. Peter stood up in the boat, full of wonder and joy.

'Lord, if it is really you, tell me to come over the waves to you!'

Jesus heard Peter's excited voice and answered at once.

'Come!'

Peter got out of the boat and began to walk on the water to Jesus. But the wind was very strong and almost blew him over, and he was so afraid that he forgot to trust Jesus, and he began to sink.

'Save me, Lord, save me!' he cried in fear.

Then Jesus stretched out his hand and caught him. 'Why did you trust me so little, why did you suddenly doubt me?' he said.

Then he took Peter to the boat, and the wind and the waves at once calmed down. The disciples knelt down and worshipped Jesus. What a wonderful Master they had!

Prayer

O Lord Jesus, whose power is without end, hear me when I, like Peter, cry to you for help. There will be many times when I think I can do things and I fail. Help me then, and do not let me sigh and give up. Reach out your hand to me, as you did to Peter, and take me close to you so that I shall not fall.

Help me to trust you, and to know that I can do all things with your help.

Amen

The twenty-sixth day

The story of Ruth

(*Ruth i; ii; iii; iv*)

There was once a good old woman called Naomi. She was sad because her husband and her two sons were dead. All she had left were the two girls her sons had married, Orpah and Ruth. One day she spoke to them.

'I am going back to the village where I was born. I must say good-bye to you both.'

But Ruth was very sorry for the old woman and did not want to leave her. She was a kind, unselfish girl, and she knew how much Naomi liked having her by her side.

'Do not ask me to leave you,' said Ruth. 'For where you go I will go, and where you stay I will stay. Your people shall be my people and your God shall be my God.'

Then old Naomi was glad, because she had felt very lonely. The two set out on their journey and at last came to Bethlehem, which was Naomi's old home.

When they arrived there, the people came out to see them. They did not know Naomi because she looked so old and sad, but when they found out who she was they made her welcome, and gave her a tiny house, just big enough for her and Ruth.

Now it was harvest time when they arrived at Bethlehem, and Ruth thought she would get some food for herself and Naomi by going down to the fields when they had been cut, and picking up stray ears of barley. This was called gleaning.

So Ruth went to the field of a farmer called Boaz and began to glean. Boaz saw that there was a strange young girl gleaning in his field and he asked his servants who she was.

'That is Ruth,' he was told. 'She has come here with the old woman Naomi. She is good and kind, and she will not leave old Naomi. She looks after her and loves her – and now she is gleaning ears of barley, to take food back to their little house.'

Boaz looked at Ruth and thought what a sweet face she had. He went to her and spoke kindly to her, telling her that she could glean with his maidens, and drink his water whenever she was thirsty.

'I have heard of your great kindness to old Naomi,' said Boaz. 'Such kindness is very pleasing to God and to men. Come to us at mealtimes and we will share our food with you.'

Boaz told his reapers to drop a great deal of barley near Ruth, so that when she gleaned she might find plenty for her basket. She took such a lot home to Naomi that the old woman could hardly believe her eyes.

The farmer Boaz grew to love the gentle, kindly Ruth, and when the harvest was over he married her. And one day she had a beautiful baby boy, who sat on Naomi's knee and smiled at her.

'Now are we indeed happy,' she said to Ruth. 'You have your reward for all your love and kindness. You have been better to me than seven sons!'

Prayer

Dear Heavenly Father, Jesus your son told us to love one another. Give me a loving heart. Let me be kind to the old and take care of them. When I am with anyone old, I will be loving and gentle, I will do all I can to help, just as Ruth did for Naomi. Help me to be kind not only to old people but to sick people, poor people or unhappy people. When I am unhappy I like to be comforted and I need kindness then. Let me give it to others when they need it too.

Amen

The twenty-seventh day

Daniel in the lions' den

(Daniel vi. 1–27)

Once upon a time there was a mighty king called Darius, and he made a strange law.

'No one shall pray to anyone but me, Darius the king, for thirty days!' said Darius. 'I shall be as God, and everyone must pray to me and me alone.'

'What shall be done to any man who disobeys?' asked his princes.

'I will throw them into the den of lions,' said Darius, 'and the lions will eat them.'

Now, when this new law was told to the people, they began to pray to Darius, as he had commanded. But one man disobeyed.

His name was Daniel, and three times every day he opened his window towards Jerusalem, the town where he was born, and prayed to God.

'I am not going to stop praying to my Lord God because the King has made a foolish and wrong law,' said Daniel, and he knelt down and prayed when he liked, not caring whether anyone saw him or not.

The princes went to the King when they saw Daniel kneeling and praying to his God instead of to Darius.

'O King, Daniel has disobeyed your law. He prays every

day to the Lord God and not to you. Shall we throw him to the lions?'

Then Darius was sad to think he had made a law that would harm a good man like Daniel. But his law must be kept, so that night Daniel was brought before the King before he was put into the lions' den.

'Daniel, may your God to whom you pray so often save you from the lions!' said Darius, sadly.

And then poor Daniel was taken to the deep pit where savage lions were kept. He was thrown down to the roaring lions, and the pit was closed and sealed up so that no one could open it until the King himself came.

The King sat grieving in his palace that night. How foolish and wrong he had been! He would not eat or drink, nor could he go to sleep because he was so unhappy about Daniel, his friend.

The next day the King went sadly to the den of lions, feeling certain that Daniel was eaten. He cried out in a sorrowful voice, 'O Daniel, servant of God, is your God able to save you from the lions?'

And then, to the King's wonder and amazement, he heard Daniel's voice coming up from the deep pit.

'O King, live for ever! My God sent his angels in the night, and they shut the lions' mouths so that not one of them hurt me.'

Then the King was full of joy and ordered Daniel to be taken up out of the pit. He was not hurt, for the Lord God had taken care of him.

And then Darius made a new and better law, which he sent out to all his people. 'Peace be unto you! I make a law that in every part of my kingdom men shall fear and worship the God of Daniel. He is the living God and steadfast forever. His kingdom shall not be destroyed, and his power shall be without end.

'He delivers and rescues those that love him, and the world is full of his signs and wonders.'

And so, because of Daniel's trust in God, all the people followed him and trusted in his God too.

Prayer

O Heavenly Father, who sent your angels into the lions' den to help Daniel, send your angels to help all those who trust in you and call for your help.

And if your angels are busy, then send me and any others who trust in you and want to do your bidding. We will help too even though we may be children, and small. There are many things we can do and we will do them. If you want a ready servant, dear Lord God, look down upon me tonight.

Here I am, send me.

Amen

The ten unhappy men

(*Luke xvii. 11–19*)

It happened once that when Jesus was walking to a village, his disciples with him, they met a band of ten unhappy men.

These men were lepers, poor creatures who suffered from a terrible disease called leprosy. They were not allowed to go near anyone else, so they had to live where they could, and trust to the pity of the villagers to throw them food.

When anyone came near they had to call out 'Unclean! Unclean!' to warn them that they were lepers.

Now, when they saw Jesus they knew who he was at once. 'See!' they said to one another. 'Here is Jesus! Look at the crowds that are following him!'

And they began to call out piteously to him, as loudly as they could. 'Jesus! Master! Have mercy on us!'

Jesus saw the miserable band of lepers. He knew how unhappy the men must be, cut off from their homes and families.

'Go, show yourselves to the priest!' he said to them. Now, people who had had leprosy were allowed to go to show themselves to the priests of the church when they were cured, not until then. So, when Jesus said, 'Go, show yourselves to the priests,' it meant that they were no longer lepers. They were healed!

The ten lepers heard his words in amazement. Joyfully they set off to find the nearest priests.

They looked down at their poor miserable bodies as they went, and to their great delight they saw that they were indeed healed. The bad places were gone, their skin was whole and clean. They were no longer lepers, feared and hated by everyone. They were whole men again, ready to work and to live as other men did.

Now one of the lepers was so amazed and joyful when he looked down at his body and found that it was healed, that he stopped in astonishment.

He could hardly believe his eyes. But it was true. This man Jesus had healed him by his words. The leper gave a great shout of joy, and, leaving the other nine, he went back to Jesus.

He sang loud praises to God as he went back. When he found Jesus he flung himself down in the dust at his feet, and put his face to the ground.

'Master, I thank you! Great Lord, this is a wonderful thing you have done for me this day. How can I find words to thank you? How can I tell you how grateful I am? You have given me back my health and happiness!'

Jesus looked down at the grateful man, and then looked after the other nine, who were now a good way away. 'Did I not heal ten of you?' he said. 'Where are the other nine? Only one of the ten has come to give thanks for his happiness.'

He raised the grateful man to his feet. 'Go your way,' he said. 'Your trust in me has given you back your health. You are quite well.'

And the man went off rejoicing.

Prayer

O Lord Jesus, who had pity for all those who were ill or un-happy, have pity on them still. Help those who are in pain, and comfort all who are sad. Bless all the doctors and nurses, all the ministers and preachers who try to bring peace and happiness to others. Thank you, Lord Jesus, for making me healthy and strong. When I am ill and get better, I will not forget to thank you. I will be like the tenth man in the story, and kneel down to give my grateful thanks.   *Amen*

The first stone

(John viii. 1–11)

One day Jesus sat in the Temple, talking to the people as usual, and healing the sick who were brought to him. He told the children the stories they loved, and they pressed round him happily.

But suddenly there was a great disturbance. Some men called Pharisees were dragging along through the Temple a poor, sobbing woman. She had done something very wrong indeed, and they had caught her, and meant to punish her.

The punishment for what she had done was a very terrible one. It was to be stoned. Any one could pick up a big stone and throw it at her. It was a dreadful punishment.

Now these men who had caught the woman had made a plan. They were pleased about it. They hated Jesus and they wanted to see if they could make him say something that people would not like.

'We will bring this bad woman to Jesus,' they said. 'And we will ask him if she shall be punished by having stones thrown at her, because that is the punishment written down in our law. Now, if Jesus says, "No, she must not be punished by stoning," we will say, "What! You would have us break the law! How wicked you are."

'But if he says, "Yes, keep the law and have the woman stoned," then we will say to all the people around, "See how cruel this teacher of yours is! He preaches love and kindness, but yet he would have you throw stones at this poor woman." '

This was the plan they had made. They thought it was a very clever one indeed. They dragged the weeping woman up to Jesus, with delight on their faces. 'Now we will catch him!' they whispered to one another. 'He cannot get out of the trap we have laid for him!'

Jesus had seen the sobbing woman. He had seen the delight on the faces of the Pharisees who dragged her into the Temple. He knew they would try to trap him, and he was sad. He was unhappy for the woman who had done so much wrong.

He looked down at the ground, and did not seem to hear the Pharisees when they spoke to him. 'What do you say to us about punishing this woman by stoning?' they asked, cunningly. Jesus was too sad to answer, so they asked him again and again.

And then Jesus stood up and looked at them. Everyone was silent. What was the great preacher going to say?

'Whichever of you here has never done anything wrong may throw the first stone at this woman,' said Jesus.

Then everyone there looked into his heart and remembered the bad things he had done. One man slipped away, ashamed. Another man went. Then another and another. From the oldest down to the youngest they crept away, ashamed, and the poor woman was left alone with Jesus, sobbing bitterly.

107

Jesus looked up. He saw nobody there but the woman. 'Where has everyone gone?' he said. 'Did no one say what your punishment was to be?'

'No one, Lord,' said the woman, trembling.

'I am not going to give you any punishment either,' said Jesus. 'Go away and do not do wrong again.'

Prayer

Dear Lord Jesus, wise and forgiving, help me never to judge people unkindly. You were always merciful and understanding, and when people were ashamed and sorry you forgave them.

Forgive me too when I do wrong things that I am ashamed of. And help me to forgive others when they also do wrong things and are ashamed and sorry. Let me never cast a stone at anyone.

Amen

The thirtieth day

Ask and it shall be given you

(Luke xi. 1–13)

One day, when Jesus had finished praying in the Temple, one of his disciples spoke to him.

'Lord,' he said, 'teach us how to pray.'

Then Jesus told him a prayer, which I will put on page 134 for you, and which you too can learn, just as the disciples did.

After Jesus had told the disciples this prayer, he told them *how* to pray.

'You must pray as if you really do mean all you say,' he said. 'You must think what you are saying. You must want what you are asking, and you must believe that you will get it if it is the best thing for you. You must never pray without thinking, or as if you did not mind whether God was listening or not.'

Then he told them one of his stories to show them what he meant.

'Suppose one of you has a friend, and you go to him in the middle of the night because you need some bread. You hammer at his door and shout loudly, because your friend has gone to bed and you must wake him.

'You call to this friend, and say: "Pray, lend me three loaves, because a friend of mine has come to me from a long journey, and he is hungry. I have no food to set before him. Please help me."

'And your friend answers from inside the house, "Do not trouble me! I've locked my door, and I am in bed. My children are in bed too, and asleep. I cannot get up and find bread for you."

'If you shout to him again and again, and beg him to do what you ask, he will know you are really in earnest, that you mean what you say, and he will get up and find you the loaves of bread and give them to you.

'So that is how you must pray. Think what you are saying, be earnest, do not give up.

'I say to you, "Ask and it shall be given you; seek and you shall find; knock and the door will be opened for you."

'Do you suppose that God, your loving Father, is not glad to give you good and happy things? Do not all good fathers like to give their children good things and make them happy?

'If a little boy goes to his father and asks him for a piece of bread, would he give him a stone instead? No, he would give him bread.

'And if he goes to his father and begs him for a fish, would he give him a snake? No father would do that.

'Or suppose the little boy asks his father for an egg, would he give him instead some horrible insects?

'Now, if ordinary fathers like to give their children good things, how much more will God, our Heavenly Father, listen to what we ask for in our prayers, and give us the best gifts that he has!'

And, after those little stories, the disciples understood better how to pray. We shall know too, and we can be certain that God, our Father, will listen lovingly to every word we say.

Prayer

Dear Heavenly Father, I have heard what your son Jesus said to his disciples when they asked him how to pray. I know how to pray now too. I shall know that you are listening, I shall know that you are glad to hear what I tell you and what I ask you. Tonight I ask you to bless all those I love and all who love me. Help me to be good and loving to my family, and to everyone I meet.

Amen

The thirty-first day

The last story Jesus told

(Matthew xxv. 31–46)

This is the last story that Jesus told. It is one of the loveliest of all.

'Now,' said Jesus, 'when I come to you again, before me shall be brought all the people of the world, every one that has ever lived. I shall separate them one from another, just as a shepherd divides his sheep from his goats.

'I shall set the good sheep on my right hand, but the goats shall be on my left.

'Then I shall say to those on my right hand, "Come, blessed children of God, enter the kingdom that has been made ready for you from the beginning of the world. For when I was hungry you gave me meat; when I was thirsty you gave me drink. When I was a stranger you took me in, and when I was in rags you gave me clothes to wear. When I was sick you visited me, and when I was in prison you came to me."

'Then my good sheep, that stand on my right hand, shall say in surprise:

' "Lord, when did we see you hungry and fed you? Or

thirsty and gave you drink? When did we see you a stranger and took you in, or in rags and gave you clothes to wear? When did we see you sick or in prison and came to you?"

'And I shall answer and say, "Whenever you did any of these things, even to the very least and poorest person, you did them to *me*."

'Then I shall say to the wicked ones on my left hand, "Depart from me into pain and sorrow! For when I was hungry you gave me no meat; when I was thirsty you gave me no drink. When I was a stranger you did not take me in; when I was in rags you gave me no clothes to wear; when I was sick and in prison you did not visit me."

'And then those on my left hand shall ask me in surprise:

' "Lord, when did we see you hungry or thirsty? When did we see you as a stranger, or in rags? When were you sick or in prison and we did not help you or visit you?"

'And I shall answer them, and say, "Because you did not do these things to those who needed your help, you did not do them to *me*!"

'Then those on my right hand, the good sheep who helped all who came to them in trouble or sorrow, shall come into my Father's kingdom, and take their place in joy and gladness; but the wicked ones, who did no kindness and showed no love, shall depart from me into sorrow and darkness.'

Prayer

O Jesus, help me to be one of your good sheep, and put me on your right hand. Let me all my life long help to feed the hungry, clothe the ragged, and be kind to the sick and sorrowful. I cannot do these things to you but I will do them to others for your sake.

And let me help those who are too blind to see that you are in the poor and the hungry and the sad; for I would not like anyone to be sent from your side into darkness and sorrow.

Amen

Special stories and prayers

The First Christmas

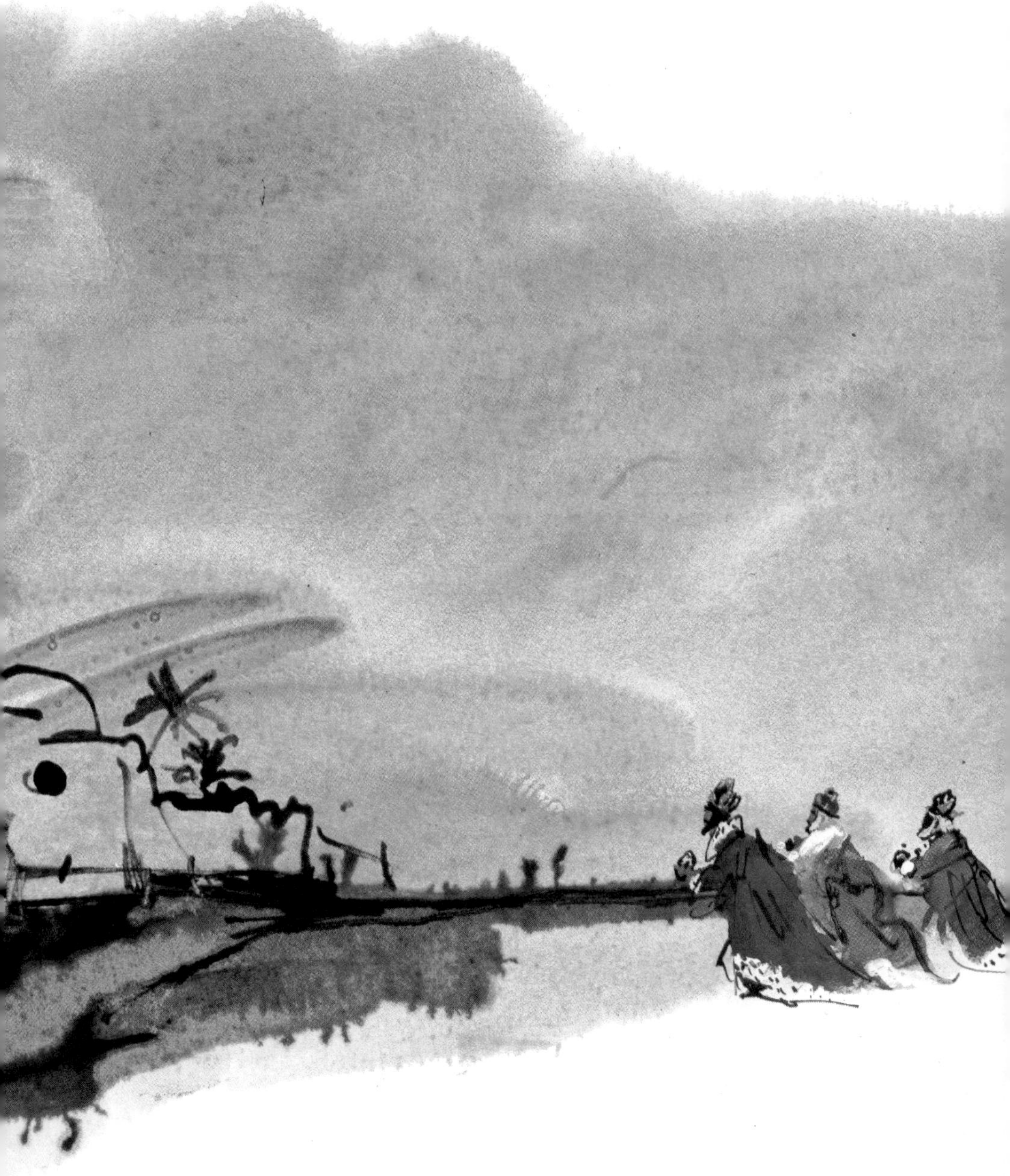

The first Christmas

(Luke ii. 4–7)

On the first Christmas Eve, nearly two thousand years ago, two people went slowly up the hill to the little village of Bethlehem. One was Mary, tired and pale, riding on a little donkey. The other was Joseph, her husband.

'Oh, Joseph, are we nearly there?' said Mary. 'I am so tired.'

'Yes, we are almost there,' said Joseph. 'Look, I can see the lights of an inn. We will go there for the night, and you shall rest. You have come such a long way and you are very tired.'

Soon they came to the inn. Its lights shone out, and merry voices came through the window. Mary was very glad that they had come to the end of their long journey.

'Ho, innkeeper!' called Joseph, and soon the man came, holding a lantern to see who the travellers were.

'Can we have a room?' asked Joseph. 'My wife feels ill and tired. We have come such a long way.'

'There is no room at the inn!' said the man. 'The town is quite full. You will not find a bed anywhere.'

'But I must find some place for my wife to rest,' said Joseph, in dismay. 'She is so very tired.'

The innkeeper shone his lantern on Mary. He was a kindly man and he was sad to see Mary's pale face and big tired eyes.

118

'There is one thing you can do,' he said suddenly. 'I have a cave at the back of the inn, where I stable my oxen. You could sleep there, if you like. It is full of animals, but I could have the place swept for you and clean straw put down for you to lie in.'

'Let us go there, Joseph,' said Mary. 'For really I cannot go any farther tonight.'

The innkeeper took them to the cave. He called his servants to sweep it out and put down clean straw. Mary lay down in it to rest.

Joseph was anxious about her. He brought her hot milk and made a pillow for her head. There was a draught from the open entrance of the stable cave, and he took off his heavy cloak and hung it there to keep out the wind.

Nearby was their little donkey, glad to have food and rest too. Beyond him the big oxen stamped in their straw. Doves slept up in the roof, and there was a warm, sweet smell of animals everywhere.

And in that dim stable, with oxen standing near, the little Jesus was born that night – the King of all the world, who was to reign in the hearts of many many men.

Mary looked down at the baby in her arms, by the light of the flickering lantern that Joseph held. 'The Son of God is here,' said Mary. 'But I have no cradle to put him in! Where shall he lie?'

Joseph fetched Mary the clothes she had brought and she put them on the tiny baby, crooning to him happily. Joseph stood near, wondering where to put the child, for he wanted Mary to lie down and sleep in peace.

'Look, Mary,' said Joseph, 'we will put the baby in a

119

manger! I will put soft hay there, and the manger shall be his cradle.'

So the little Jesus was put in the manger on the hay, and soon fell asleep. And Mary slept too on the straw, happy that her baby had come.

That was the first Christmas, when the little Christ Child was born, and ever since then we keep Christmas as a day of happiness and joy – and we remember how he came to Mary long long ago in the stable of the inn at Bethlehem.

Prayer

Dear Lord Jesus, tonight is Christmas Eve; and I am remembering the very first Christmas of all. I wish I could have peeped over Joseph's cloak at the doorway of the cave, and seen you as you lay in Mary's arms. I would have liked to come in and touch your tiny hand. I would have liked to put hay in the manger for you to lie on.

Thank you, dear Son of God, for leaving the glory and beauty of heaven, and coming down to our world to share with us all our joys and sorrows. Tomorrow is a joyful day, your birthday. We cannot give presents to you so we will give them to one another.

You will keep your birthday in heaven, dear Lord Jesus, and we will keep it here on earth, with loving thoughts and deeds.

Amen

The shepherds and the angels

(Luke ii. 8–21)

Now, when Jesus, the little King of the world, was born in Bethlehem, the angels in heaven sang loudly for joy.

They had been keeping watch over the village, and when they saw Jesus in Mary's arms, they wanted to tell the great news to somebody. But who was awake in Bethlehem? The tired people were fast asleep, and nowhere was there a light to be seen.

But out on the hillside beyond the town there were shepherds guarding their sheep. They were awake, because they were watching for wolves. Beside them were their dogs, watching too. The shepherds huddled together, their cloaks round them because they were cold. Now, as they sat talking, a great light came in the sky and all around them, a light so dazzling that the shepherds were afraid. What could shine so brightly in the middle of the night?

Then they saw a beautiful angel standing nearby, in the middle of the light. He shone too so that they could hardly bear to look at him. Then the angel spoke and his voice sounded like great music over the hillside.

'Fear not; for behold I bring you good tidings of great joy, which shall be to all people. For unto you is born this day a Saviour, which is Christ the Lord. And this shall be a sign unto you – you shall find the babe wrapped in swaddling clothes and lying in a manger.'

The shepherds could hardly believe their ears. For hundreds of years men had watched and waited for a Saviour, the Son of God, who would come to help them and to teach them – and now this angel was telling them that the Saviour was near at hand in Bethlehem.

They gazed at the bright angel in wonder and joy. Then suddenly the dark sky opened, light came through, and, all above and around the first angel, there appeared a great crowd of shining beings. There were angels everywhere, and they all sang joyfully.

'Glory to God in the highest, and on earth peace, good will towards men!'

And then, as the shepherds listened and watched, the dazzling light faded away, and the angels disappeared. The dark sky came back again, and only the faintest echo of the song reached their ears. 'Glory to God . . .'

For a while the frightened shepherds said nothing. Then they began to whisper to one another. 'Those were angels we saw! The first angel was the most beautiful of all.'

'Were we dreaming? What did the angel say?'

'He said that the Saviour had come to Bethlehem. We should find him in baby clothes, sleeping in a manger!'

'Then let us go and look for him. We *must* find him. But where shall we look?'

'The angel said he was in a manger. We must go to stables then, because that is where mangers are. But how strange that the King should be lying in a manger!'

'We will look in the stable of the inn. Sometimes the inn-keeper lets travellers sleep there if all his rooms are full. Let us go!'

So they went to the inn, and when they saw the lantern light shining dimly from the old stable cave at the back of the inn, they went there.

The shepherds found Joseph's cloak pinned across the doorway. They peered over it – and there, lying in a manger, in baby clothes, was a tiny baby.

'There he is!' said the shepherds. 'Before our very eyes! Let us go in and worship him.'

So they went into the stable, and there they told Joseph and Mary about the angels and their song.

Mary took the sleeping baby from the manger and held him in her arms. The shepherds knelt down before him and prayed. Here was the Saviour of the world, the King the angels had sung about. How wonderful!

Then the shepherds went and the stable was quiet again. Mary bent over the little Jesus.

'You have only a manger for your cradle, and hay for your covering,' she whispered, 'but angels from heaven came to sing when you were born. Sleep peacefully, little King of all the world!'

Prayer

Most loving Jesus, King of all the world, we have kept your birthday today, we have rejoiced because it was Christmas Day. Long ago the shepherds came to worship you in the stable. They knelt before you and honoured the Baby King. I honour you too, and as I kneel before you tonight I will say what the angels said to the shepherds. 'Glory to God in the highest, and on earth peace, good will towards men.' Amen

The First Good Friday

The story of Good Friday

(*Luke xxiii. 26–47; John xix. 16–30*)

And now tonight comes the saddest story in our book.

Jesus was taken to prison because his enemies said that he had been upsetting the people, and had been saying that he was their King.

For his punishment he was to be nailed upon a cross of wood and left there till he died. Two robbers were also to be put upon crosses beside him.

The crosses were made of two heavy pieces of wood. One was a long piece, to be driven into the ground. The other was a shorter piece, the crosspiece, that was nailed across the first.

Soldiers put the heavy crosses on the shoulders of Jesus and the two robbers, and told them to carry them to the hill outside the town.

Jesus was tired and weak, and he stumbled under the weight of his cross. Every time he fell down the soldiers made him get up again. But at last they saw that he really could not carry his cross, so they looked about for someone else to do it.

There was a man watching called Simon of Cyrene. A soldier caught hold of his shoulder. 'Carry this man's cross for him,' he commanded, and Simon was forced to take it and carry it for Jesus. He carried it all the way, and Jesus was able to walk faster.

And then, alas, the soldiers nailed Jesus to his cross and the robbers to theirs.

The robbers turned to mock at Jesus. 'You say you are the King of the Jews, the Saviour of the world. Then why do you not save yourself and us too!' cried one of the robbers.

The other robber looked at the patient face of Jesus, and he was ashamed. 'You and I have done wrong and are being punished,' he said to the first robber. 'But this man has done no wrong.'

By the cross, weeping bitterly, was Mary, the mother of Jesus. John, one of the disciples, was doing his best to comfort her. Jesus saw them both and was sad. Who would look after his mother for him now? And who would comfort John?

Jesus could have pity on others, even when he was in great pain and misery. He spoke to them both. 'Behold your son!' he said to his mother. 'Behold your mother!' he said to John. Then Mary knew that she and John must be like mother and son; and it was so, for John took Mary to his home and treated her kindly as if she were really his mother.

Then Jesus gave a loud cry. 'Father, into your hands I entrust my spirit!' His poor head drooped and he said no more. Jesus of Nazareth, great healer and preacher, teller of stories, lover of little children, had given up his life.

'Truly this was a good man,' said the captain of the soldiers near the cross. 'I think he must have been the Son of God.'

Prayer

Dear Lord Jesus, it makes me sad when I hear how cruel people were to you so long ago. You did no wrong in our world, you healed those who were sick, you brought happiness to sad people, you did nothing but good. And yet you were nailed upon a cross with two robbers.

I would have tried to carry your cross for you, if I had been there. I would have helped you if I could. But I was not there, so I will try to help you now, and carry your cross by helping other people for your sake.

Amen

The story of Easter Sunday

(Mark xvi. 1–8; John xx. 11–18)

On Good Friday you heard the sad story of how Jesus was nailed to the cross and crucified. Now hear the glad story of Easter Sunday, when he rose from the dead, and showed himself to those he loved.

That Friday was a terrible day for his disciples and friends. They could not believe that their beloved Jesus, so good and noble, had been put to death. The disciples hid away in fear, grieving bitterly.

Saturday went by, and Sunday came – and very very early that day, just as the sun was rising, a little group of women went to the cave in the garden where the dead body of Jesus had been placed.

They brought sweet spices to anoint the body of Jesus. As they went they remembered that a heavy stone had been rolled over the mouth of the cave.

'Who will move it for us?' they said to one another. But when they got to the cave they saw that the stone was not there. Someone had rolled it away. The women were astonished.

They went inside the cave. The body of Jesus was not there, but the women saw, sitting at one side of the cave, a young man in a dazzling white robe. Was he an angel? The women were very frightened indeed.

'Don't be afraid,' said the angel. 'I know that you have come to find Jesus, who was crucified. He is not here. He has risen again, as he said he would. See, this is the place where he was laid. Now go quickly and tell his disciples that Jesus has risen from the dead. Tell them that they will soon see him again.'

The poor women listened, trembling. Then they turned and ran from the cave. They must go to the disciples and tell them the great news. Jesus had risen from the dead!

Now one of the women who had followed Jesus, the one called Mary Magdalene, also went, weeping, to the cave that

morning. She saw that the stone had been rolled away from the cave, and she bent down to look inside. Jesus was not there – but instead she saw two angels, one sitting where Jesus's head had lain, and the other where his feet had been.

She could not think who they were or why they were there. Then one of them spoke to her. 'Why do you weep?' he said.

'Because they have taken away my Lord and I do not know where they have laid him,' said Mary.

And she turned away, half frightened, to go back. But there, behind her, she saw someone standing. She could not see who it was because she was blinded by her tears.

'Why do you weep?' he asked. 'Whom do you look for?'

Mary thought he must be the gardener.

'Sir,' she said, 'if you have carried him anywhere, tell me where you have laid him, and I will take him away.'

But it was Jesus himself!

And then he spoke one word so lovingly that Mary at once knew him.

'Mary,' Jesus said.

Mary turned to him at once, her heart full of joy. 'Master!' she cried gladly, and fell on her knees before him. He was not dead! He had risen again, and would go to his friends and comfort them tenderly, before he went to his Father in heaven.

Prayer for Easter Sunday

Dear Lord Jesus, this is a joyful day, because it is Easter Sunday, the day that you left the dark cave and went to show yourself to your friends who thought you dead. You died for us, so that we might know you loved us and wanted us to be good. All the angels in heaven praise you, and all who love you want to sing your praises too. Hear my voice among them all, dear Lord Jesus, for I love you and praise you as much as any angel in heaven.

Amen

Your own prayer

When your mother has read you the story and the prayer at night, you will like to say your own prayer. You will want to pray for the people you love, perhaps you will want to ask God's special help for something, or you may feel that you have time to remember more people than usual. So you will make up your own prayer, and put into it whatever you like.

Here is a prayer to show you what I mean. It was said by one of my own little girls when she was small like you. She made it up herself, just as you will make up your own each night too. You will not say what she said, of course, because every person wants to say a different prayer. This is what she said one night some years ago:

'Dear God,

It has been a lovely day. Thank you. Thank you for the lovely time I had on the river, and for the swans I saw. Thank you for my dog and our two kittens. Bless Mummy and Daddy and our baby and Nanny and Lorna and Auntie Dorothy and the gardener, and the postman and don't forget Granny and Grandpa. Bless my dog and the two kittens, and the little robin that comes to bathe in the pond. Bless everybody in the world, and look down on me and bless me too and help me to be good. Amen.'

The Lord's Prayer

This is the prayer that Jesus taught his disciples when they
asked him how to pray.

Our Father,
Which art in heaven,
Hallowed be thy name.
Thy Kingdom come. Thy will be done
*   on earth, as it is in heaven.*

Give us this day our daily bread.
And forgive us our trespasses, as we
*   forgive them that trespass against us.*
And lead us not into temptation; but
*   deliver us from evil:*

For thine is the Kingdom, the power, and
*   the glory, for ever and ever.*
*   Amen*

And this is what the Lord's Prayer means

Father of us all,
Who lives in heaven,
Help us to love and honour your name.
Let your great Kingdom of Love spread over all the world,
And help us all to do what pleases you here on earth, as it is
*   done in heaven.*

Give us all we need for this day.
And forgive us the wrong things we do just as we forgive those
*   who do wrong things to us.*
Do not let us go into any place where we might do wrong.
But save us from all harm and danger.

For yours is the Kingdom of Love, and all power and glory,
*   for ever and ever.*

*   Amen*

Three graces

Choose which you like, and say it before meals.

Here I sit upon my chair,
Fold my hands and say my prayer,
Hear me Jesus, while I say
Thank you for my food today.
                    Amen

Now I sit down at my place,
Bend my head and say my grace,
God bless the food that here I see,
And God bless all who eat with me.
                    Amen

Thank you for the world so sweet,
Thank you for the food we eat,
Thank you for the birds that sing,
Thank you, God, for everything.
                    Amen

A lovely old hymn

You may like to say this on Sundays.

God be in my head and in my understanding,
God be in my eyes and in my seeing,
God be in my mouth and in my speaking,
God be in my hands and in my doing,
God be in my feet and in my going,
God be at my end and at my departing.

A morning prayer

You can say this every morning if you like it.

Thank you, dear Lord Jesus, for watching over me all night long. Now, in this new day, help me to be good and kind, and bless everyone I love.
Amen

An evening prayer

You can say this when there is no time to read
your story or hear the prayer for the day.

Thank you, dear Lord Jesus, for my happy day. Forgive any wrong thing I have done. Watch over me tonight as I sleep, and bless everyone I love.
Amen

A prayer for when I am ill

Dear Lord Jesus, look down on me today, and comfort me. Whilst others run about and play, I am in my bed. Help me, dear Lord, to be patient and cheerful, to be as little trouble as I can, and to be grateful for all the kindness around me. Please let me get better soon.

Amen

A thank-you prayer for getting well

O Lord Jesus, comforting and kind, I have been ill, but now I am well. I have lain in my bed, miserable and in pain, but now I am up again, happy and glad. Thank you for making me well. Thank you for making my legs strong enough to walk again. Thank you for all the loving care that has been given me, and the kindness everyone showed to me. Let me return it to them when they too are ill or in pain.

Goodnight, dear Lord Jesus. Keep me forever by your side.

Amen

A prayer for when I have done wrong

O Lord Jesus, today I have done wrong. I will tell you what I have done . . .

Now I am sorry and ashamed. Forgive me and let me show you that I will do my best to make up for the bad thing I have done.

I know that you will always forgive those that are truly sorry. Thank you, dear Lord Jesus, for forgiving me. Now I can be happy again, and tomorrow I will be good.

Amen

A New Year's Eve prayer

O Lord Jesus, tomorrow is New Year's Day, the beginning of a New Year for me and everyone. Now help me to make my New Year promises and to keep them all through the year.

What promises shall I make? To be kind and loving, to be truthful and honest, to be generous and fair. Help me, Lord Jesus, to keep every one of my promises, and to make this New Year a happy one for all my family.

It is a new beginning, and I will put away the bad things that belong to the Old Year, and welcome only the good and lovely ones.

Amen

A prayer on a birthday night

O Lord Jesus, one more year has gone, and another year lies in front of me. Thank you for all the happiness in the year gone by, and thank you for my lovely birthday and all its presents and cards. Today has been my day and I have been happy. Help me in the new year that is in front of me now. Let me grow up healthy and strong, good and kind, and let me walk by your side all the years of my life.

Amen